"Here Rae Diamond (the healer behind the text of the wonderful *Cantigee Oracle*) frames space where paradox softens, outsung by a note that gathers all sounds into itself and rings out repair. They persuade us that this sound, this felt space, is the availability of a home, a site charged for them by their experiences without one. 'Homeless' and 'unhoused'—the first offers a binary, the second points to process, to potential, to risk of loss and risk of gain. The words do not struggle to replace the other in their diction; they work throughout with sous rature and grayed-out print. These and other names, notions, goads clash and chime, abide as in acoustic space . . . All bones are ear bones? Bone-deep, listen to Rae Diamond."

—ERIK EHN, AMERICAN PLAYWRIGHT

"*floating bones* is a migratory almanac, a drifting and lyrical meditation on home and belonging. Built with poems of ineffable sonic awareness and tender, hand-drawn sketches, floating bones follows a narrator who has left one home for another, just to find that the new home is unlivable. Reckoning with this new liminality, they discover ecstatic communion with the burgeoning natural world around them. This everywhere is gulls, foxes and owls; curmudgeonly herons at the shore and seals in the water—all of this life constantly slipping into each other, seeming to skip from realm to realm. The poems in *floating bones* are a spiritual dance with a nature constantly rebecoming something else, giving certainty to uncertainty. Diamond's awareness of our temporality, our 'tempo/rarily animate fragment(s)' of existence, turn this book into a revelation. *floating bones* is the sacred book by your bedside that you turn to before you sleep. In a time of housing crisis, environmental displacement and global uncertainty, Rae Diamond is a profound guide through the unknown future."

—EVER JONES, AUTHOR OF THE *TRANSLIBERATORY LYRIC NIGHTSONG* "*floating bones* is a work of exquisitely crafted poems that excavate and question the meaning of home with honesty and vulnerability. As the reader enters the book with its foreword in poetic form, they learn 'when at last I found / a home it felt less / like home than everywhere…' Skillfully constructed poems abound with images that reference nature and mortality and musical language that compels: 'still outside in/twilight hush in/spiritshattter in/ windstir in/awe a drifting/pool reflecting/the world back/to itself.' This book does, in fact, include a skeleton full of gorgeous and mysterious illustrations of found animal bones, deer hooves and antlers, and human teeth with wings. Diamond, an interdisciplinary artist, brings their practice in the visual arts, music, and performance to the work which creates a mesmeric experience for the reader. This startling debut by Rae Diamond offers the reader a portal to a formally inventive and revelatory poetic space in which to reside."

"Rae Diamond's collection shows how reality, even belonging, is 'poised for adaptation.' With exquisite form that turns language into sleight of hand, this genre-defying work shook all the language in my body until I was a collection of bones rattling in a jar and reminded me that home is nowhere and everywhere."

"There's an ethereal quality to Rae Diamond's poetry that guides a reader somewhere that is both familiar and forgotten. In our hasty realm of societal promises and comforts, *floating bones* offers an invitation to drift awhile in order to experience the dynamism and magnitude of the natural world that lives beyond our familiar walls."

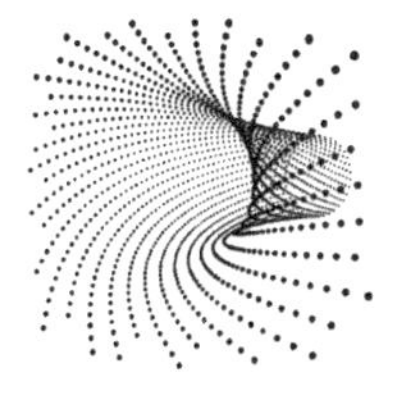

FIRSTMATTERPRESS

Portland, Ore.

floating bones

ALSO BY RAE DIAMOND

The Cantigee Oracle

floating bones

a dialogue of belonging

rae diamond

FIRSTMATTERPRESS
Portland, Ore.

First Edition

Published in the United States
by First Matter Press
Portland, Oregon

Paperback ISBN 978-1-958600-06-1
Library of Congress Control Number: 2023943355

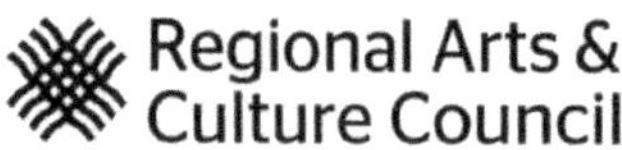

This literary arts project was funded by Regional Arts
and Culture Council's Arts3C Grant Program for
Creation, Cultivation & Community in the Portland
metropolitan tri-county region. www.racc.org

Editor: Emily Moon
Contributing Editors: ash good & Lauren Paredes
In Cohort: Charity E. Yoro
Contributing Readers: Hailey Spencer & Riley Danvers
Copy Editor: Andra Vltavín

Cover Illustration
Copyright © 2023 by Lara Rouse
@good_luck_lara

Book design by ash good
ashgood.com

FIRSTMATTERPRESS.ORG

. . . there were no flowers,
so I started picking up bones.

Georgia O'Keeffe

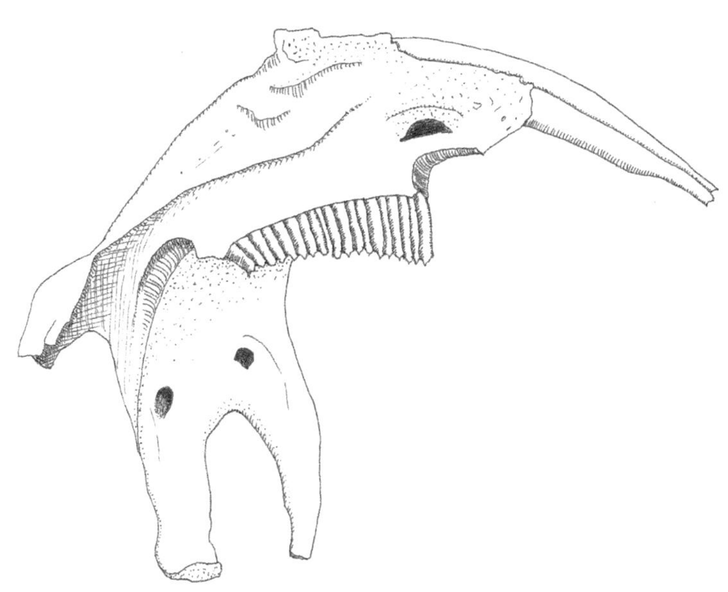

contents

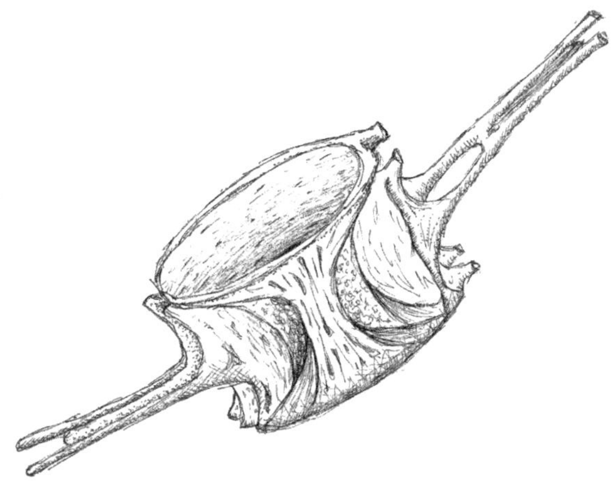

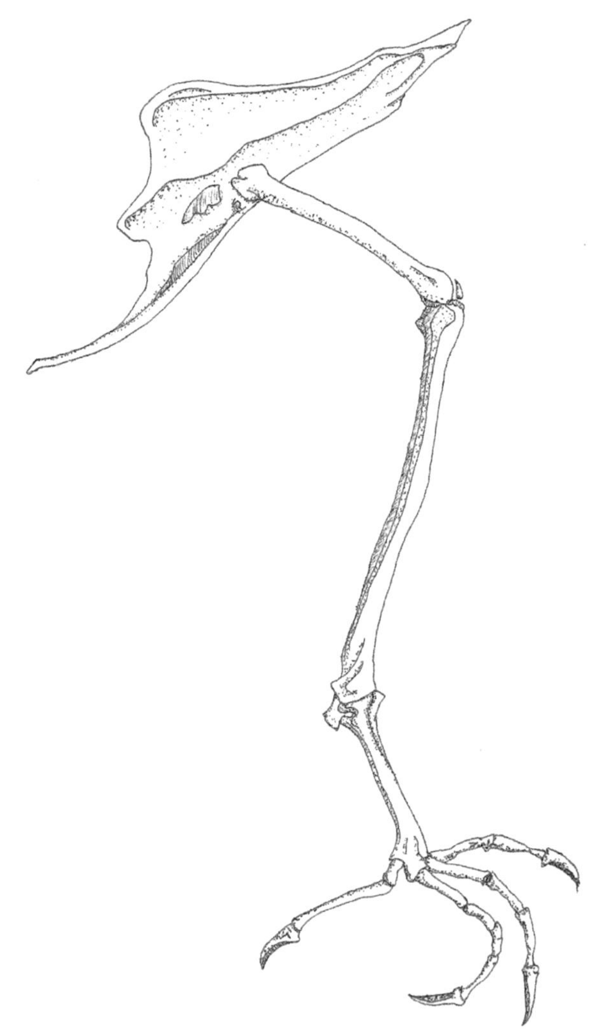

foreword

welcome

may you feel at home
        in these pages
                pages written when

i was without a home
                    when only
                                unseen doors opened for me
                    when everywhere was a door and
                    when at last i found
            a home it felt less
            like home   than everywhere
        come
            in
                come
                    in
                        come
                            in

last drink

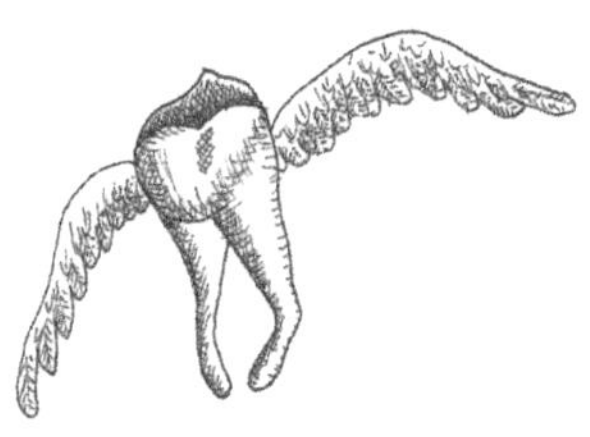

leaving this land
the person i have
been here condensing
into a camera
receiving all reflected
light imprinting
not as memory
but as food
a nutriment
to savor in lean times
to come in the inexorable
cycles of growth and
decline now dissolving

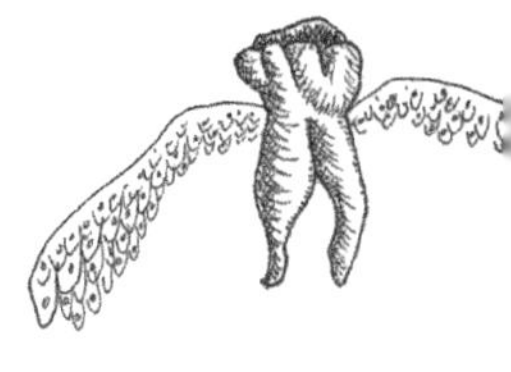

into a dry mouth
drinking with fervor filling
its body at some known
source before
at once departing from
the well well known
and entering into
an elsewhere
that spans in all
directions beyond this
here that exists only
now and can never
be returned to

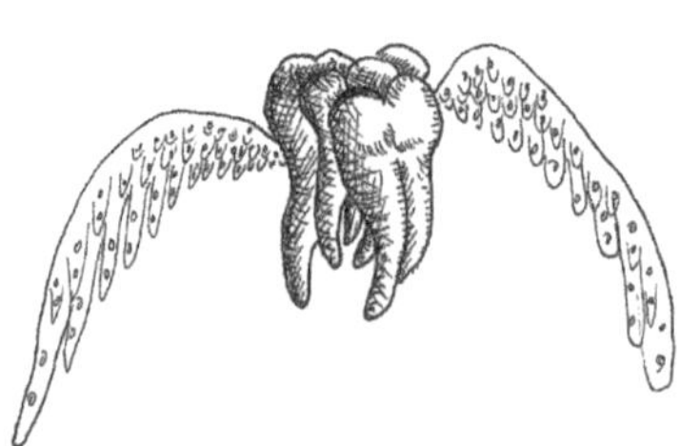

~~what kind of nourishment do you receive~~
~~only in your~~ home

windstepping

here in the center of this sleeping street looking
      for northern lights instead seeing first meteors
         now deer on rear hoofs eating apples

here on this square of salted turf reaching
      for effulgence from above bricks and clouds
         now soles like lanterns shine into loam

here leaning over this stark drop to the sea
      for the feeling of windgust unhinging feet from edge
         now windstepping down wood stairs to pebbled sand

here among this shimmerrhythm of frogs singing
      for eggs to fructify a chorus of continuation
         now troubles flux into rapture

here before this silver leaping fish searching
      for a language for this unlit spiderstrand blink
         now adhering now dispersing

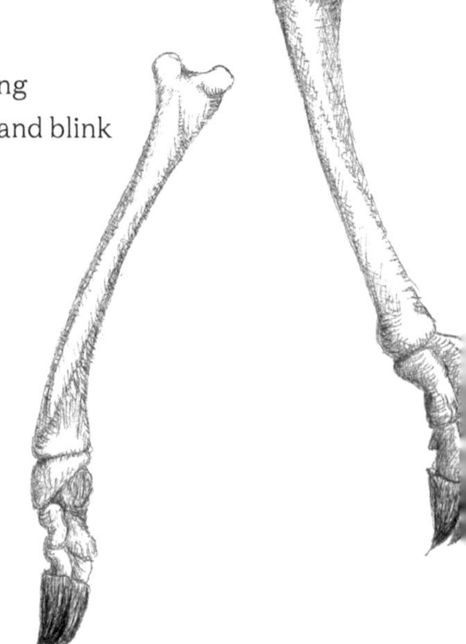

tentative **filament**

a chipmunk protests
my presence as a hummingbird
hovers before me a song
of suspicion thrumming in
scintillant speedblurred wings

upon my approach deer
hooves clatter over pavement
then surge into thorned
thickets of undergrowth
as two barn owls shriek to one

another across a span
of field lit by a wide moon
the sky is swallowing
in increments once
devoured it will be

spit out a silver sliver
pointing east over
this place where a door
opened enough for me
to enter a humble observer

of this exquisite weave
of lives weather light
space where i wonder if
i might be received a modest
thread in this breathing cloth

helix of exhalations

>   this   dimness before
>   dawn strung with dewed webs
>   then   spiders repair rainbows
>
>   this   morning hoof
>   prints in the sand
>   then   deer on the beach
>
>   this   white sun in the mid
>   muddle of day
>   then   a red horizon
>
>   this   daybreak not met
>   by ritual bird trills
>   then   songs in the gloaming
>
>   this   night a meteor
>   illumines an arc of sky
>   then   forever withdraws its radiance
>
>   this   listening witness is
>   here is here
>   then   gone

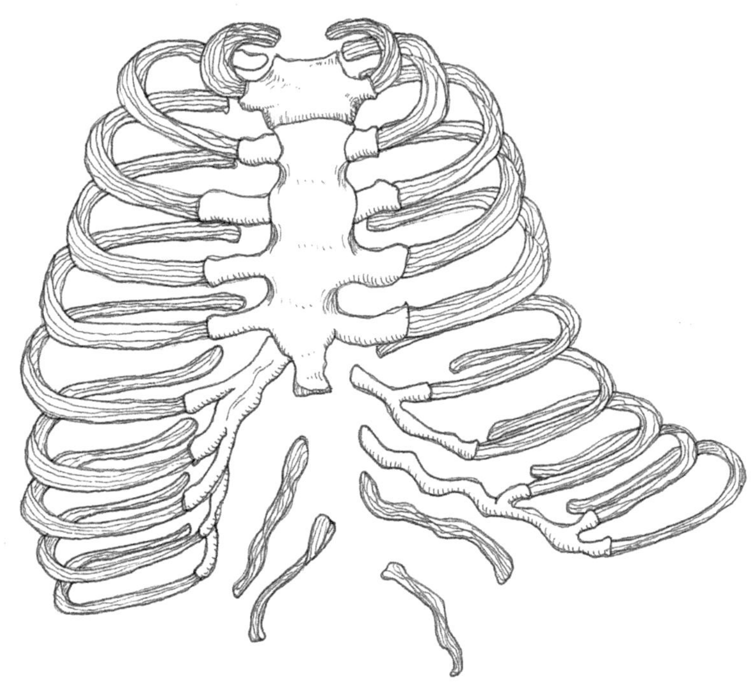

~~how does your breath shift~~
~~when you return~~ home

blue now

now   but earlier
the   mountains   glowed   the
mountains pink
pink   the   moon close
to full   close
to this   living
           rock   in the relative
distances of   its ellipse
           its yawn   ing oval
its tilted spiltcircle
           whirl   and i a tempo
rarily   animated   frag
ment   stepping   oh
oh   over   boulders
bold or stand under   sky
no   step   stepstep
past dead thorned   branches unhitching
from fabric stretch   ahead to the next
wet   stone to   the next sea
kissed   rock slosh
to the left twig   tangle
to the right rocks   drop into be
yond   the reaching
steps   on stones   in time
onto   sand
seasoaked   receding

                              receiving foot sin
                 king   sinking at each
                 step   and the old
lady   behind   me
shouting   arms wa
ving   in the air
you   did it you did
                              it and i did

but   there was
another   stretch
of   ocean   against
rock   to clamber
                              over under
the dimming   dome   in
the darkening   air   and i made a way
i cannot call   mine   over that
                              rockreach too but

beyond   her   elated
                 eyes
it was   some   act no
one   wit
nessed   a nest of   experiences lost
that might   someday
hold an egg   or two   a clutch
in a roost   a clasp
on a boot   and

        maybe   wings will
fallow then   follow   wind and arc
    above   and away   and ah
      ah   a way

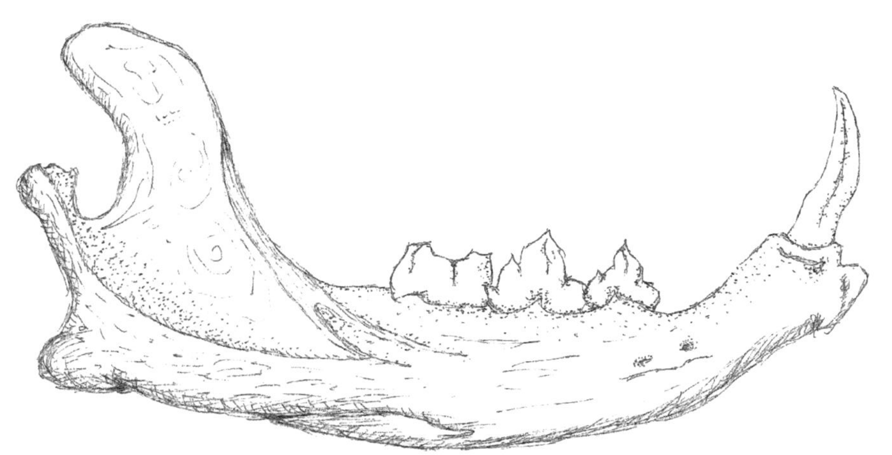

wing through walls

it   is   okay   not
to   have   a   home
made   of   walls
full   of   things
f   a   m   i   l   i   a   r
all   that   lies   beyond
the   walls   and   comforts
of   others   becomes
an   open   field
of   inhabitable   spells
in   which   one   is
struck   by   all
the   breath   of   the   world
brings   now   rain
now sunscorch   now
honk   of   goose   now
dogwag in boat   now
wary   gaze
of passing eyes   now
smileshy   child   now
still   outside in
twilighthush   in
spiritshatter   in
windstir   in
awe   a drifting
pool   reflecting

the   world   back
to itself   clouds and
the winged ever   passing
t   h   r   o   u   g   h
now   spark   speckled
darkness   now blue
                    be
                              yond

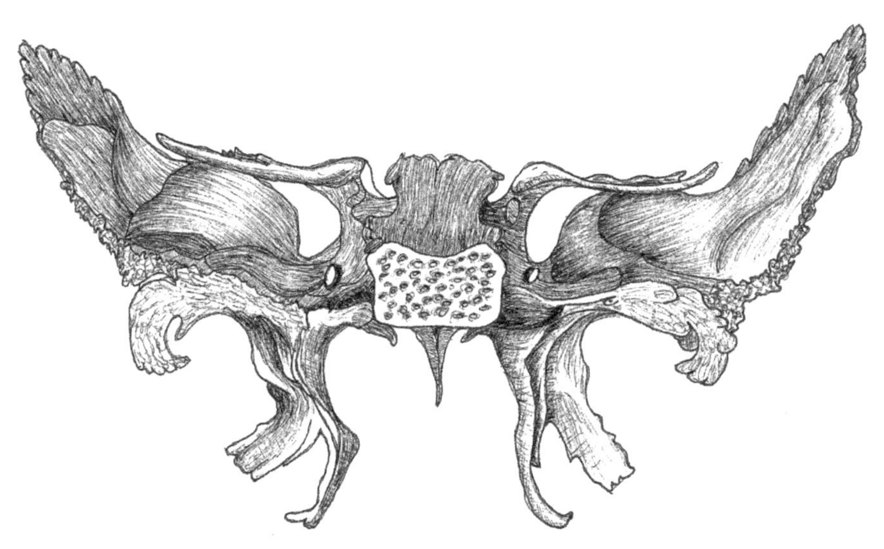

~~what emotions are safe to feel~~
~~only when you are~~ home

enchanted telephone

i   am   assembling   an   empty

          space

if i toss

                  you a can

                  on a string

a   c   r   o   s   s   its fathomless span

                  you

        might hear

me metallic

        sing into tin

        re

          ver

        ber

          ant

from an obscure   edge

at dusk   deft bats

             might

     careen

t   h   r   o   u   g   h

echoecho

        locating insects

i

might

pierce

t h e   e x p a n s e

with

blown

glass

marbles

in

order

to

lose

orbs

in

void

crystal spheres encircling

swirls

of

color

might appear

in   your   tin

if you rattle them

the can could

become

a jar

the marbles

fireflies

together a lamp

and

the bats

collecting

clouds

of storms

to come

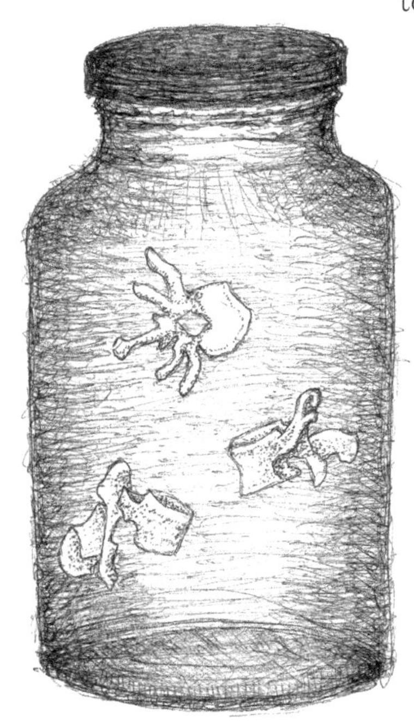

nucleus of zero

22

there is an aperture i   o p e n
step through be   come the sky evenings blue and
pink embrace of plastic   flamingoes overlooking tangles
of garden as the sun   and olympics meet
the space where manic   moth wings rise papery where
round antlers of deer emerge   covered in velvet then extend
sharpen harden into branches   of animate spears or in the early
hours i am falling sky   luminous grey permeating vapor
obscuring mountains erasing   distance blurring sources of
sound into one chord of   immersion ship horn gull
cry truck brake one   omni amoeba engulfing
each cell each atom   filling spaces between
all nuclei and e   lectrons the worms
and the   holes   through
which they travel

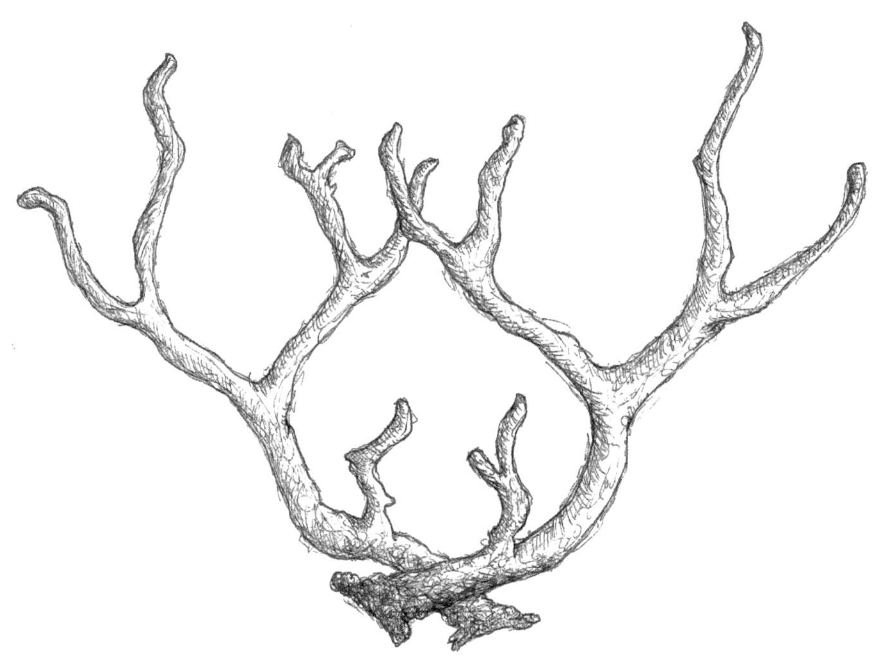

every home ~~has a heart~~
~~a place one is drawn to~~
~~where~~
        is
        ~~the~~
            ~~heart~~
        ~~of~~
        ~~your~~
home

applause for the alone

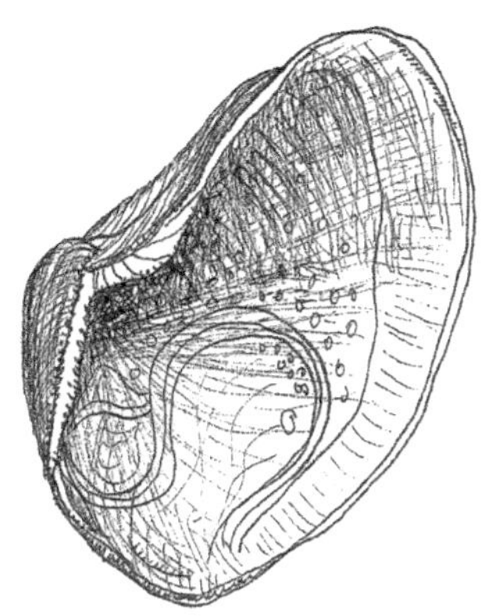

stripped spine of a gull feather
echoes sky the color of crumbling

shale above moist earth receiving then
resisting feet stepping on tree seeds

cedars flank this trajectory in dark
green memory creamed

with the slow rush of gusts
that touch only moonkissed tips

a low sound in a high space
hemlocks look on

unspeaking
up ahead in concrete ruins

doorways gape between expanses
of grass and shadowed underworlds

where a single note sung becomes
a sonic kingdom lingering

just beyond the last pass of air
up larynx and out lips

clap hands here and the walls
clap back clapback clapba

your head is opening

opening a copper peony
on a stalk of neck above
a xylophone of heron bones
surrounding your thorax
poplarlike pointing starwards

with lethal beaks birds set
drum bones spinning thrumming
a clacketing virrrr rrround
your parallel urribs your
interpulsing heart lungs

as a buzzbunch of bees
bumble dances the dust out
from under your diaphragm
sweeps it away a toxic pollen
brings back honey to lube

your creakity knees stuck
in subservient bend yessir
yessir no more now sweet
sashaying into flamingo
tinted sunrise you drink

into eyes thirsty for new
light that slides like a smack
of pink jellyfish down the red river
of your throat into a blood blue
cacacacardiac ocean of iron brine

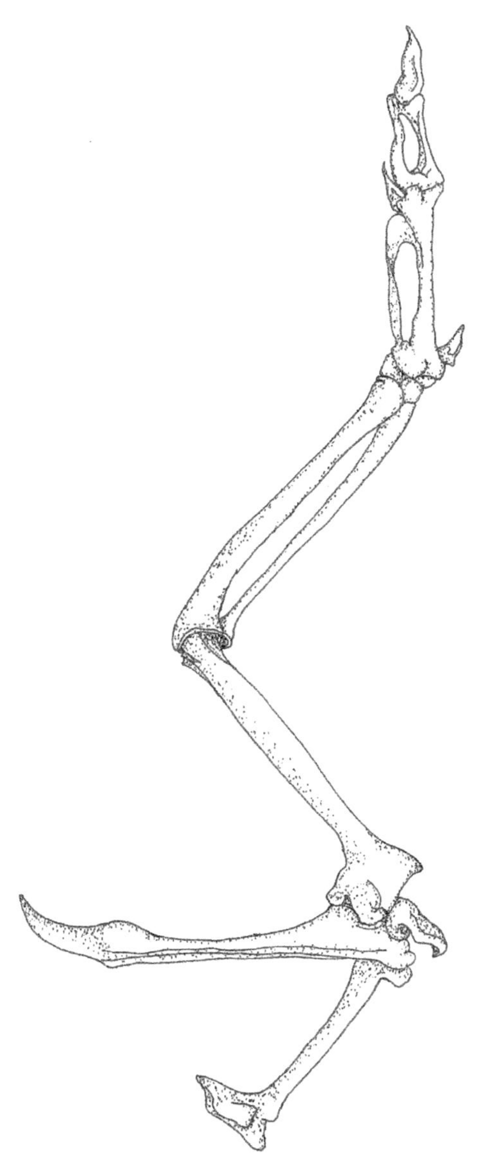

~~what does it feel like~~
~~in the heart of your~~ home

star walking

home is where the feet are
the feet are on the earth
sometimes on concrete
or floors of wood of
plastic of shag
the feet
made of stardust
are wrapped in wool
in cotton encased in cork
in rubber the feet trade
weight and space with each
other a game they play
called
      walking
            or
                  they
                        may
share air until
s u d d e n   u n i s o n
thud on earth
the feet
are tucked sometimes
against thighs and
shins in a universe called
s i t t i n g s t i l l i s i m p o s s i b l e

a   nowhere   in
which   to   notice
how   everything   is
moving   how   there   is
no   discernable   edge   and
yet   there   is   a   center
a   cynosure   to   which
the   feet
at   once   stellar   and
h   o   m   e   b   o   u   n   d
are   tethered

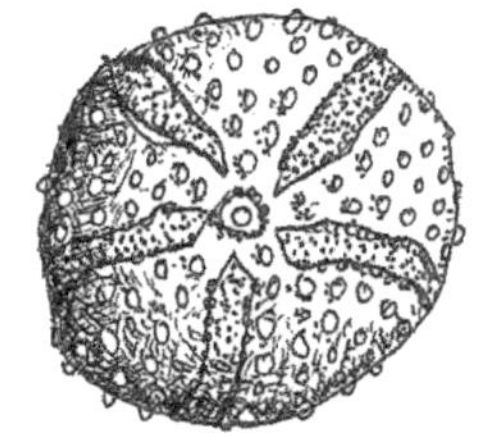

what does it feel like when you step
in the door of your home
and close it behind you

with no home be

     a gull
          step webbed feet over
          slick stones
          span slender
          wings on curved currents
              wobble
          float   dive
          buoyant in biting brine
              distance   dissolves bird
                      form into voices
                      chortles
              screeches
        songs
   cries
              sounds without name
              inhabit
              pass through
              shift between
                environs
                tongues
                modes
                            present
    poised for adaptation

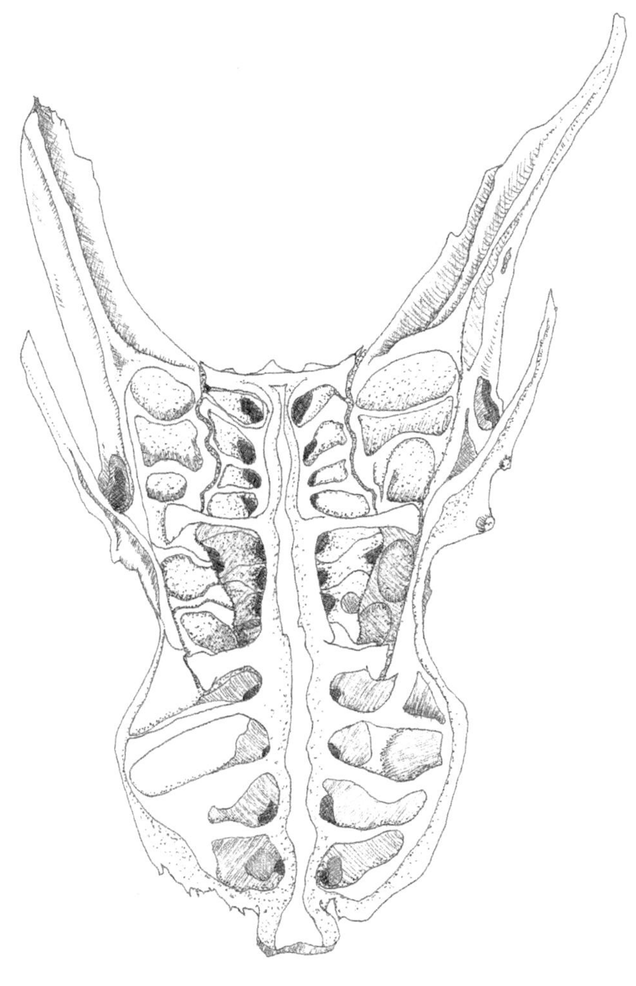

we will echolocate this moment

we will take the path of swit
chbacks that cross cross cros
ses itself we will wind twine of
lions mane along its inter
secting edges to form a leonine web hum
ming with ionic tension we
will run bows of horse
hair against gut
of cat play
in counterpoint with bird
trills the song about the two
lil babes who lost their
way we will play until gnats
form living comestible clouds
for bats to feast on in vectors of mem
brane flight that parrot in air
the crosshatch of our earth
en way our sound will swell
as frogsong emerges from gul
lied dips radiant as dis
tant eruptions of orbs of gas
in epic space we will tune
ourselves to the trajectories of inter
locking waves of amphibian
and chiropteran chirps echo
locating us all within
the space of a kairos win
k

~~what ways do you take care of yourself~~
~~only when you are~~ home

housing crisis

              i
         walk
           down
                the
                    hill
                       to
                          the
                             water
                          a seal surfaces
                          continues to rise

                in air into

e x p a n s e s   a   b   o   v   e
                          this peopled place
                            not like a bird
                                        flying
                        like a hot air balloon
                          some warm mass

f   l   o   a   t   i   n   g

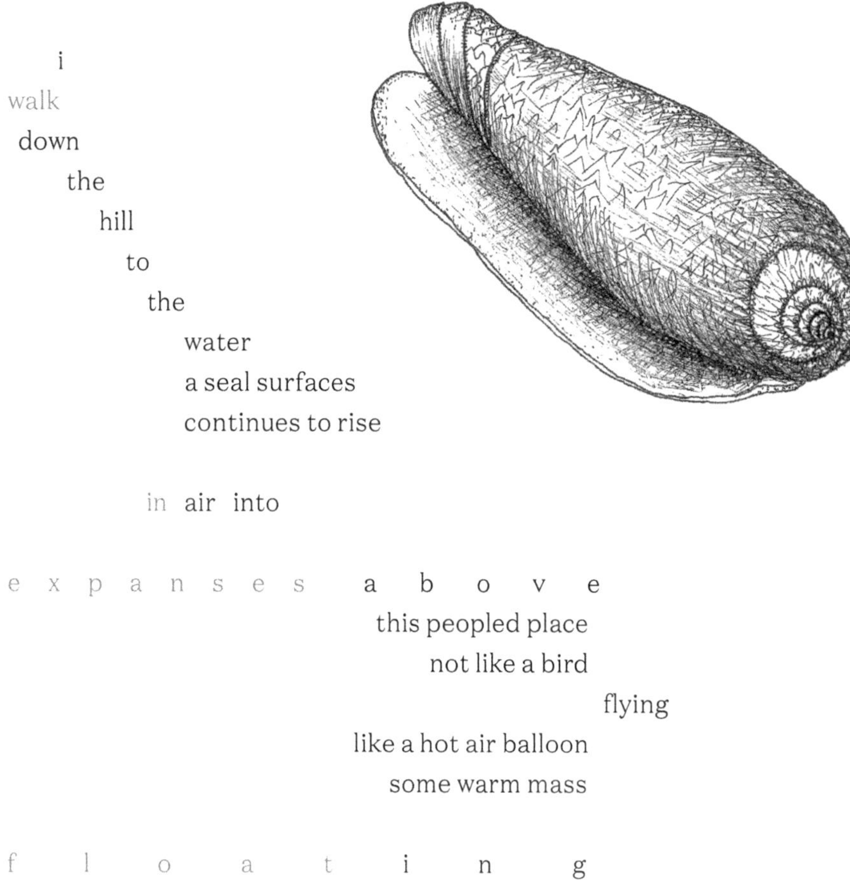

untroubled
on
cool
cur
rents
thin
n
e
r
than the fathoming
of these eyes that
w   a   t   c   h
until seal becomes speck

in distance
it remains
unknown whether
and how
the seal returns
to the sea and i
to some earthen abode

ashes ashes we all

spill epic
and
angular rays
of rising
in a   sun
cloud   from an
early   aperture
today and
yesterday
peers into   an eyeless fish
some   head
and upping   beyond
in the   beyond
beside   wakes of   sight on
creosote   kayaks and   a dock
ooze   foghooting   downing
forever   frozen   ferries
drip   in time
but never   sticky
quite   dark
fall   rivulets
into
the
sea

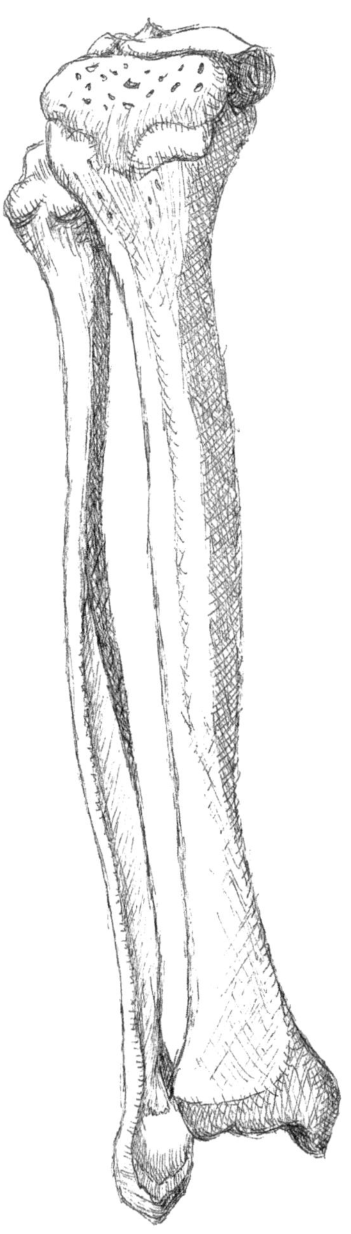

as we all will

lost in dirt circles in
the park that was an art
illery corps in a forgo
tten time i sing a song to a friend
on the phone as a fox
watches from the under
brush i follow at a di
stance until its trail shrinks
too low too narrow for a two
legged one singing a downcast
song about one endowed
man who shared food with his
peers but not with a star
ving fellow and what be
fell each when they
died as we all will some
day you me my friend the
fox all of us and still
this moment spirals in
me when a pair of mating
beetles buzz about me a few
nights later and before i can re
cover from that carnal wonder
a moth and i collide goldglo
wing in an amber lamp beam be
fore parting in darkness and the next
day while still in the rapt
ure of this pearl string of phenome

na i hear the familiar and who
            lly unexpected ruh ruh rhythm
                    of horse hoofs clippity
        clomping up the pave
ment behind me and i
            turn to lo see yes a horse trit
                    trit trotting beneath a man
        in chaps and a straw hat
i wave in an effort to be
            polite despite my unswer
                    ving gaze the man unblin
        king unsmiling eyes glazed waves
back rides on and the herons squawk
            over the mud flats and
                    a stranger claps as i
        leap over salt streams of low
tide and come sunset i am still astoun
            ded as i eat rasp and blue
                    berries from an old jar found di
        scarded in long thirsty grass that is
sure to green in winter rains

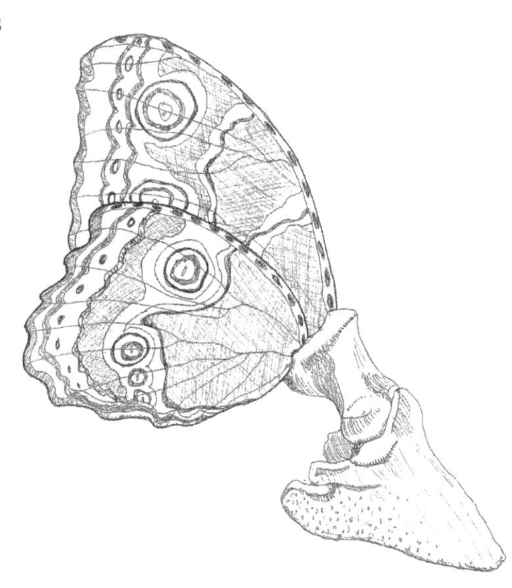

~~how do you like to unwind~~
~~once you get~~ home

      tender laplap of inlet
      water polyrhythmic against tethered
      docks and moored boats

   flap and clang of ropes
   resonant against bare masts

       curmudgeon squonks
       of the heron who owns
       the sand spit trilling
       gulls inhabit without possessing

    rushed expulsion of held
    air of surfacing seals preceding
    melodic liquid ripples centripetal
    over luminous supersurface realm

feet step hollow taps on
wood distant thunder rolls
on metal protracted crunch on stones
presssnapcrack on dry roadside
weeds not yet softened by autumn rains

        passed by rushrumbles
        of motordriven vehicles

passing by swishtwigsnaps of startled
beings unseen in undergrowth

approaching the growing solo
of a whocooksforyou barred
owl with its descending
glissando finale who

                    oo
                        oo
                          oo
                            oo

                    that fades as the unalarmed
                    banshee screeches of a barn
                    owl swell into consistent
                    intermittent prominence

                        that settle into   hovering
                        counterpoint duet at a distance
                        with the ostinato duple
                        rhythm of rubber soles
                        upon pavement steady low

                quiet and close

            continuing until weighted
            rubber hits stone steps then
            wood deck then ceases

as metal jangle of keys
preludes roll and clunk
of turning turned lock

owl rasps accompany and continue beyond
creaks of openingclosing door

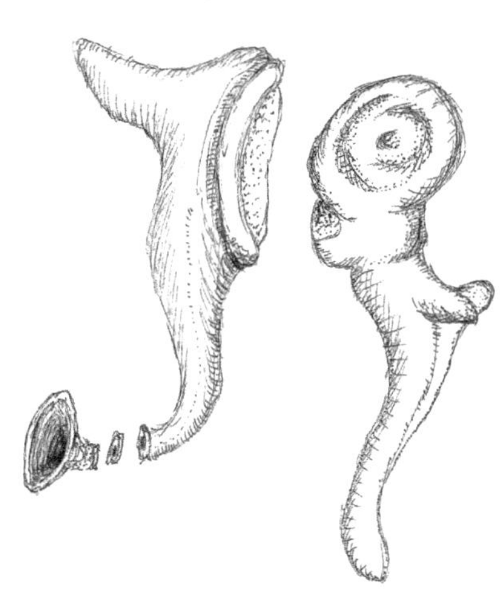

reflection flection

       listening

             listening

                until the sound

i

  am

    drops

into the pool of all

    that is

           is

              merges

with its surface

          cess

without

      any

        ripple

           of

      negotiation

          ation

              becomes the silent

mirror

      reflecting

             the din of

confusion

into

    endless

        less   space where worlds

unfurl and end

        end   lost

in the illusion of   forgetting

               what

   they emerged

        merge   from and will

return to

        turn to

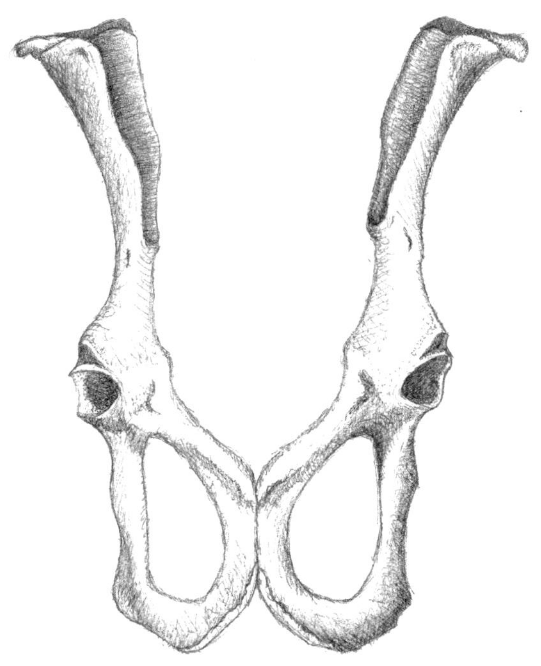

just this cloud of gnats
gnats that dart in all di
rections though the cloud
of gnats hovers in
one pulsing space
when the wind gusts
the cloud widens when
the air stills the cloud
condenses just this gnat
mass and a heron on
a protrusion of sub
merged semidecom
posed poplar trunk just
a heron and its perch re
flected the apex face card of
the mucky lagoon deck
jack of herons jack of furious
squonk at blank sur
face of water that refu
ses to cough up any fish to
day just algae just pond
scum just heron gua
no streaming white
from feathered bottom dis
appearing beneath slick mur
ky surface just

still water just water
bugs and the sub
tle ripples of their
wee feet just de
parting heron lowslow
flapping away just one
week until i leave all
this having only just

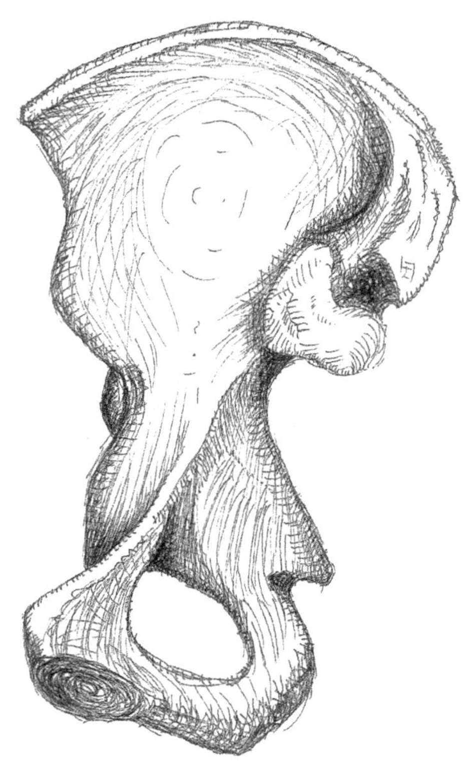

~~what do you miss about your~~ home
~~when you are away from it~~

end of summer

muted lavender clouds haloed in cool
glow precede a periwinkle sunset
        no scarlet no pink no orange no indigo no gold no
          green though you breathe invisible rainbows

overhead a gull not a gull
           an otter in a coat of white feathers
             enjoying a lofty view

insects franticflutter upwards at sundown
cumbersome cousins of ants
         beeline down in desperate diagonals
          collide with sparkling pavement
         jaggedstumble dazedbedraggled

schools of slim blue fish
submerged choreographic clouds
        wash up on the beach one stormy morning
         now you know they are not silver

two otters in oily otter coats
one parent one pup
          emerge from surf revel in sand
        slip into the sea before town dogs come

mussels squirt skywards from mud
                              clouds observe untouched

lone heron here
                                              lone heron there
                      engrossed in sequestered fishrich shallows

pearlescent fish flopsplash outinto water
              slick surface explodes into shifting shapes and sounds
                  settles returns to its quiet work of concealment

a crow on a post eyes a pair of alpaca gloves
flies off with one teal mitt in its beak
                    glove erases into atmosphere as crow becomes
                              dark pulse blot speck nothing

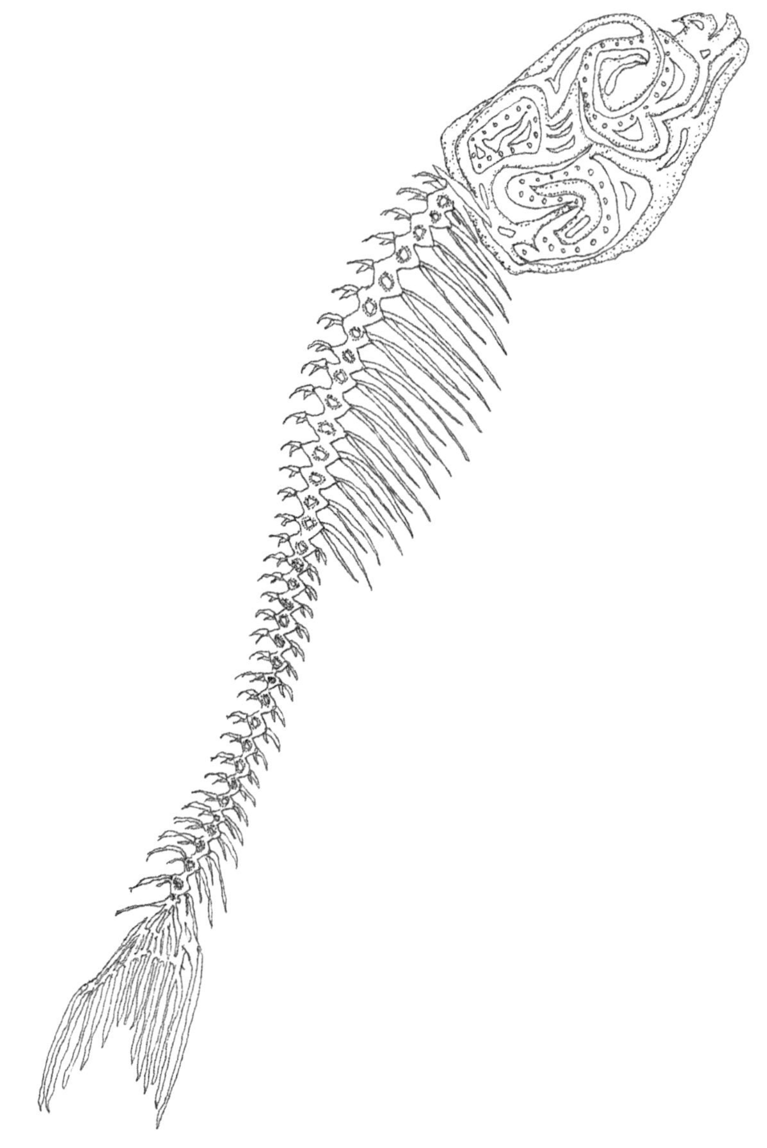

this here

conifers circumscribe
a piece of sky   that seems to arc
above a door   i enter and exit
each day the tapering   evergreens form an edge
living lace that descends   into layers of ligneous
growth this field of   sky fades in and out
of brightness and light   lessness stippled with speckles
of luster it seems   defined by distance
by trees by this door   and the walls the door
leads to but there is   no end to this heaven
not contained by solid   forms but holding all
that is here   and remote
beyond reckoning

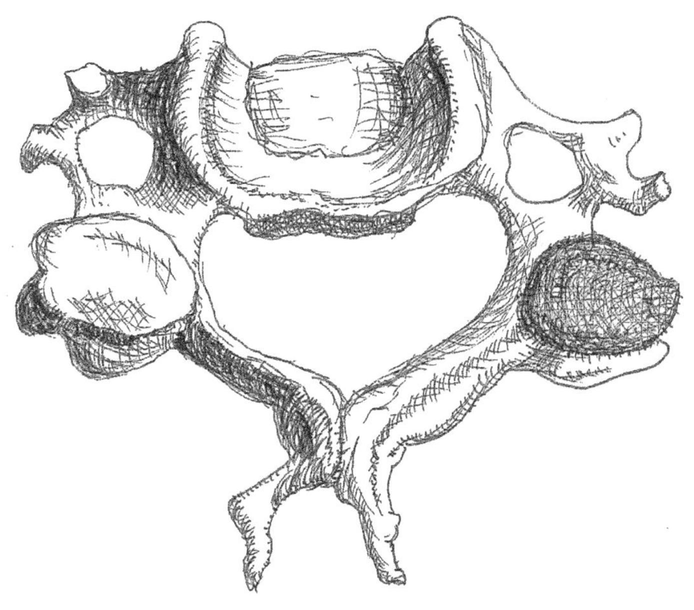

~~does your~~ home
~~love you back~~

on the last morning

gulls **emerge dark** against grey gleam
where did the white of their feathers **go**
swallowed into the mist that **swallow**ed
the sky the mountains the islands

what is visible **in the distance**
a string of **faint** pearls of light
still **ghosts** orb above where
a dock **beckons** on sunlit days

dear reader

<pre>
        poisepause

            please in this

            moment this choice

                                    linger
                                        in
                                            mystery

                                    disperse
                                        mystery
                                            into story

        linger
            close
                the book
                    step
                        outside

        or
            read
                on
</pre>

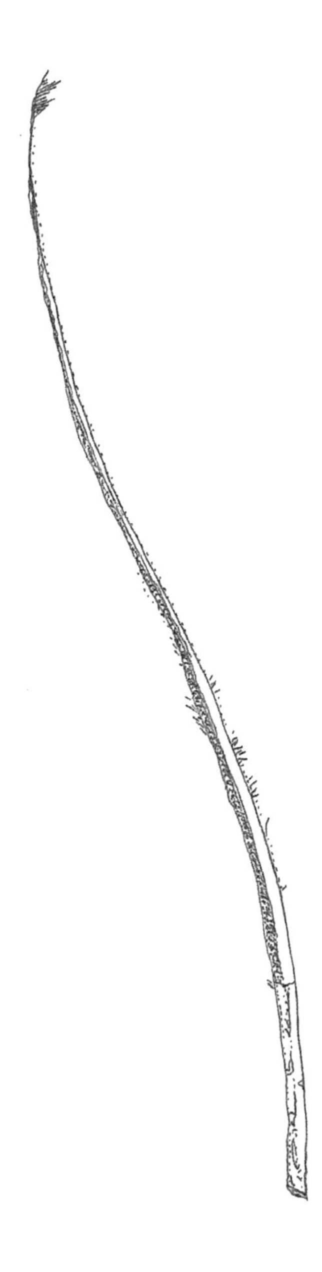

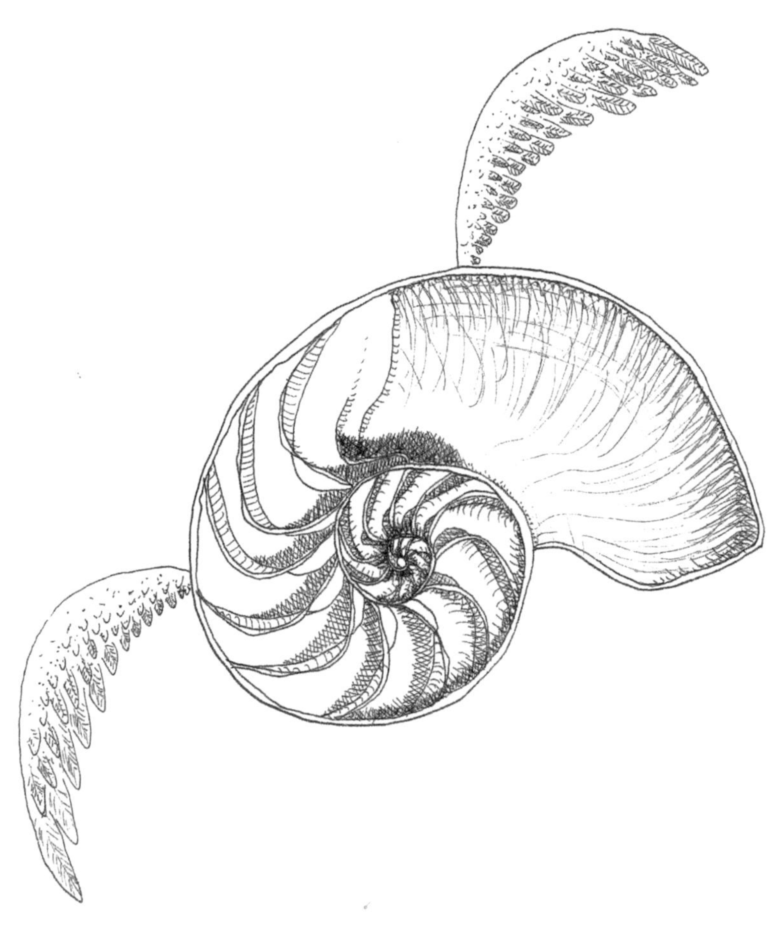

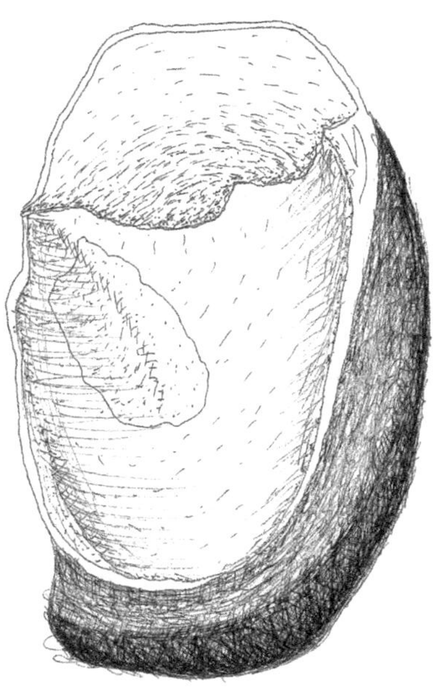
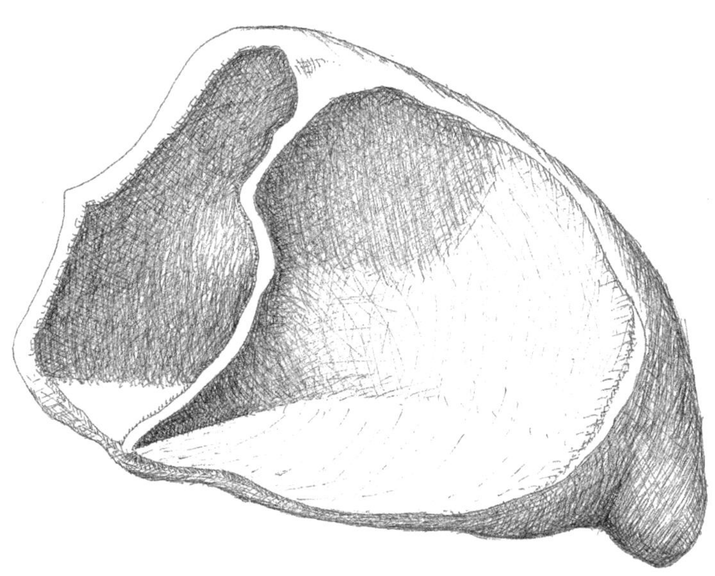

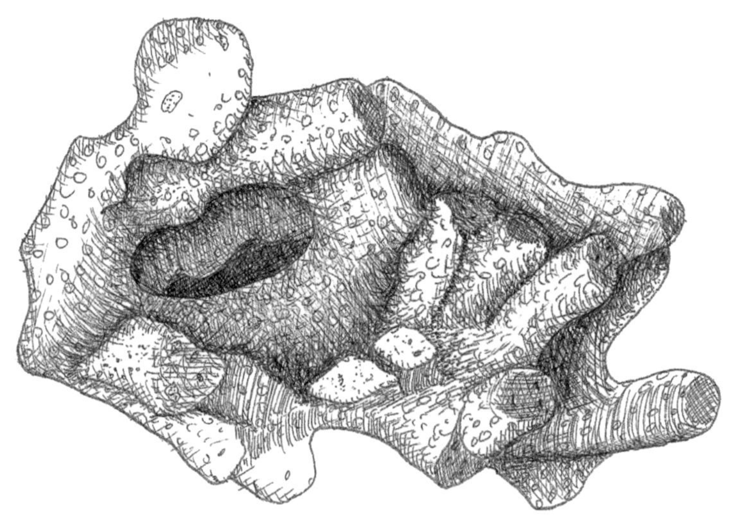

dialogues of belonging:

Our first home is the liquid space of the womb within our mother's
body. We develop in dialogue with this liquid and with the body
and being that contains it. We take up more and more space in our
mother's womb until there is no more space left for us. Then, this
singular and intimate dialogue ends and gives way to a new dialogue
that is complex and lush with possibility. We have no choice then but to
take up space somewhere on the diverse earth of this shared planet.

We do not choose where on this planet we are born. My mother was
born in a house her father built in Fiume, Italy (now Rijeka, Croatia)
during WWII. When the war ended, boundaries were redrawn. My
family's land was seized, as it had become part of Yugoslavia. They
moved to a refugee camp in a dilapidated castle and then struggled
in various parts of northern Italy until they were able to immigrate
to the United States, where my mother would eventually meet my
father. My father's grandparents were Ashkenazi Jewish immigrants
who fled the pogroms in their homelands of Poland and Russia. Their
ancestors, in turn, were displaced long ago from the Middle East.

My forebears, both immediate and distant, moved to someone
else's homeland because they were not safe or supported in their
own. Over time, the land referred to as the United States became

the home of my ancestors, and the home of their descendants.
In this wide land, some people own multiple residences and some
people have no homes, neither as property, nor leased to them.
In the midst of this lopsided situation referred to as a housing crisis,
I have found myself unhoused in a land that once gave sanctuary
to my homeless ancestors.

Like water poured into a vessel, we fill the spaces we inhabit, and
therefore, the spaces we inhabit and their conditions shape us. We
might harden into a space, like ice. We might settle into a space,
like water. We might permeate a space, like vapor. It is a dialogue.
Depending on our needs, desires, and proclivities, we change our
spaces to direct the way they shape us. We fill them with warmth,
not just from heaters, but from those things that stoke our inner
fires. This enables us to feel fluid and at ease in our spaces. We
cool our spaces if they are too warm, both with refrigerants
and with structures that help us to stay firm in our resolves and
responsibilities. We contrive our spaces so they best support our
development in the ways we want to be shaped.

Whether we own a deed or not, does the land we live on belong to us?
The belief that the land is ours implies that we are free to shape it
in whatever ways suit us best, regardless of how that might impact
other beings. We then whittle and reform the land to support us in
having a particular experience that is not yet present, generating a
monologue inspired by a future-based ideal.

What if we do not have the resources to control our climate so that
it might shape us in a beneficial way? What if we are inhabiting

someone else's space, in which they have created a climate that benefits them, even though they themselves do not dwell there?

And what happens if we have no space of our own to inhabit? What if our only space is the shared space of outside? Then the conditions of the land, climate, culture, and season shape us. We might freeze into a patch of ice on the ground that others step carefully around. We might melt into a spreading puddle, reflecting the sky. We might drift as a cloud, amorphous, with one eye on a planet full of locked doors, and the other eye on the uncontainable vastness beyond the Earth's atmosphere. We are ice, puddle, or cloud until the conditions around us change. Ice inevitably melts. Water inevitably hardens or evaporates. Vapor inevitably condenses and falls. Without sufficient shelter, the world shapes and shifts us according to conditions beyond our choosing.

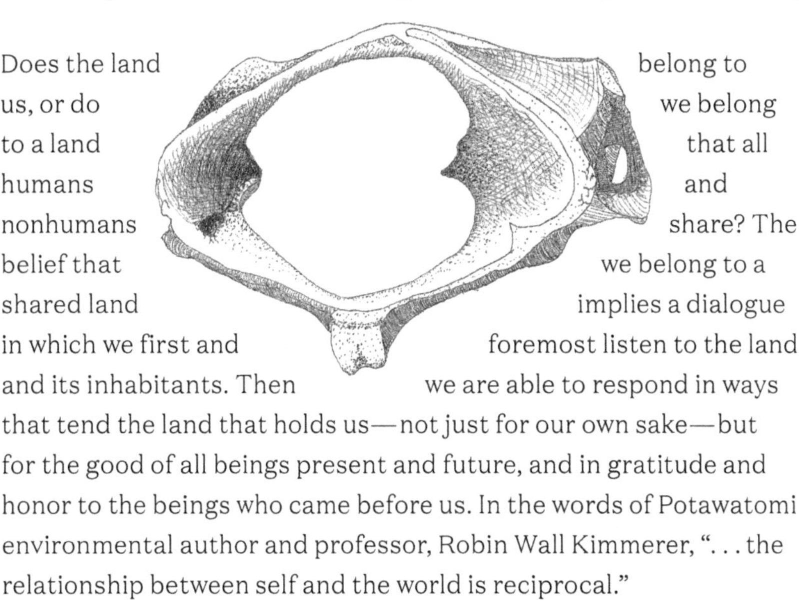

Does the land belong to us, or do we belong to a land that all humans and nonhumans share? The belief that we belong to a shared land implies a dialogue in which we first and foremost listen to the land and its inhabitants. Then we are able to respond in ways that tend the land that holds us—not just for our own sake—but for the good of all beings present and future, and in gratitude and honor to the beings who came before us. In the words of Potawatomi environmental author and professor, Robin Wall Kimmerer, ". . . the relationship between self and the world is reciprocal."

Throughout the world, most of us live on land once inhabited and tended by Indigenous people, who have since been displaced and/or cloistered into less economically valuable regions. Indigenous cultures and the pre-industrialized agricultural and nomadic cultures of all our ancestors flowed with their land and the changes that unfolded there through time—spreading over it like pools, permeating it like vapor, and blanketing it with the stillness and quiet of snow, depending on the conditions of the season and region. And just as lakes, rivers, springs, and rain nourish and make fecund the land upon which they lay, flow through, emerge from, and fall upon, this interdependent way of life enriches the land that supports its inhabitants. This is a dialogue between people and place, based on devoted observation of changing patterns of circumstances that seeks and maintains a mutually beneficial interdependent shaping.

We see this echoed in the ways the land and water shape each other. Dips in the land hold water. The deepest and vastest hollows contain oceans. Ocean waves erode rock cliffs. Rivers follow the contours of the land and, over time, reshape those curves.

What happens when water is obstructed and cannot flow freely? Some areas flood, while other areas become parched and undernourished. This has a rippling effect on the environments and inhabitants of those regions. Water is an essential nourishment for life. So is the land that holds water—that holds and houses all of us.

Where is housing obstructed? How and why is it not flowing freely, accommodating all inhabitants of this vast blue-green globe? Is it because of gridlocked permitting processes, too few builders, and limited building supplies? Is it because those with more resources are giving proportionally less money to the government, which stymies the government's ability to help those with little or no resources? Or is it because we have forgotten our common origin?

Although we are no longer in the liquid space of a womb—feeling the breath and heartbeat of our mother rippling through amniotic fluid against our skin, and through our own movements, sending ripples back towards her tissues—we are nonetheless sharing the womb of this planet's turf and atmosphere, in dialogue with it and with each other. Although we cannot feel it so viscerally, each action we take ripples outwards, touching the air, the planet, and all its inhabitants. All the other beings and the land itself ripple back at us.

What is the land saying about the affordable housing crisis? What is the land saying about the cloistering and devaluing of Indigenous peoples and their interdependent ways of life? What is the land, in this time of undeniable climate change, saying about the conversations we are having with it and with each other?

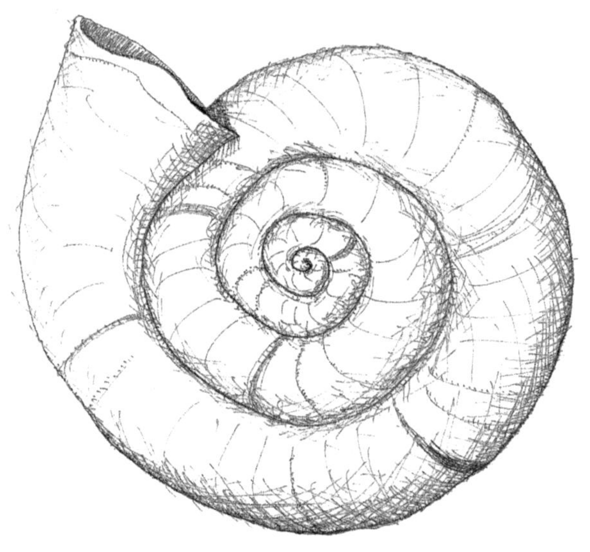

end notes

An index of illustrations, bone poems and *notes*.

doors everywhere everywhere

leaving this dissolving source   elsewhere spans beyond

This poem was written the day before I moved from my home in the Bay Area to a cabin I had rented on the Washington peninsula after a video tour and a couple conversations with the owner. I felt like I was leaping into the void, but I had no idea how true that would turn out to be.

step in center instead of reaching   drop into this lit dispersing

tentative presence blurred into lit sliver of wonder

helix of dewed rainbows prints on the horizon   this ritual of ever listening

lose distance   step over sky into receding air   an ocean beyond lost   wind a way

I chose the jaw bone of a cat because it suggested mountain peaks to me. Two and a half weeks before I moved, my cat passed away, so I was raw with grief for her during the time I was unhoused.

page 16   "wing through walls"—human sphenoid bone

no walls inhabit breath pass drift reflect wing through dark beyond

I chose the human sphenoid bone for this poem because it looks like a strange winged creature, which was how I felt in the times I have been without a home. And yet, we all have a sphenoid bone. It is utterly common, though we cannot see it. Just so, being homeless filled me with a sense of being invisible and yet right there; alien and yet utterly human.

page 19   "enchanted telephone"—human vertebrae as lightning bugs

fathom obscure echo in circling color become a lamp come

page 22   "nucleus of zero"—deer antlers

embrace wings merge velvet hours fall luminous into space

page 25   "applause for the alone"—found mussel shell

alone seed green sound speak in shadow of air

page 26   "your head is opening"—bird wing bones

opening bones point starwards drum your heart of dust into flaming ocean

page 29   "star walking"—found sea urchin shell

home is made of stardust wrapped in weight and space tucked in a universe untethered

page 32   "with no home be"—gull pelvis

float between

*I admire gulls for their versatility. I chose the pelvis of the gull
for this poem because they are visually stunning, and because
pelvises are bowls set upon the legs, holding the rest of the
body. Bowls, being vessels, contain potential.*

page 34 "we will echolocate this moment"—human scapulae as bats
echo this moment play with living clouds vector across
emerge radiant tune to waves in space

*The song mentioned is an English folk song, "Babes in the
Wood." Two young children become lost in a forest and do
not survive. There is a disorientation that comes with being
lost, making the path to safety all the more subtle and easily
missed. Robins spread leaves over the children's bodies and
sing over the place of their demise. Life is tenuous without
proper shelter. I sing this song as a reminder that even what is
most vital may die, and yet the song of life continues.*

page 36 "housing crisis"—inherited oliva porphyria shell
walk in expanses float in unknown turns

*The shape of this shell reminds me of a seal. It belonged to
a beloved aunt, who was a poet, and the first person in my
family to move to the Washington peninsula.*

page 38 "ashes ashes we all"—human tibia and fibula
spill today into forever

*The drawing of these bones has the same frozen dripping
quality as the creosote in the poem.*

*The tibia is a powerful pillar that supports us, but it in turn is
supported by the slender fibula. Being without a home feels like
walking around on fibulae with no tibiae.*

*When most people think of the word, "bone," they think of the
long bones of the legs and arms. Hence, I felt the tibia and
fibula were good illustrators of the mood of this poem with
its observations of death, both present and pending. Bones
outlast the rest of the tissues of the body, so they resonate as
symbols of what eventually becomes of us all.*

page 40   "as we all will"—horse hoof bones with moth wings

all in circles   sing low   share this parting string of waves over
strange streams of green rain

*The song mentioned is "Dives and Lazarus," an English folk
song based on a parable from the New Testament. Wealthy
Dives shares food with his friends, but refuses to share
food with starving Lazarus and cruelly drives him off his
property. Later, their circumstances change and they both
grow sick and die. I sing this song as a prayer of generosity,
as a reminder that all comforts and discomforts are—in the
greater scheme of nature—fleeting, and as an assertion of our
ultimate equality as temporary beings sharing this planet for
a moment.*

page 43   "orbit of ears"—human ossicles

orbit in rhythm with surfacing realm   step soft
be who fades into quiet continuing   then turn turn open

*These are the smallest bones in your body. They would sit
spaciously all together on the tip of your pinky finger.*

page 46   "reflection flection"—feline pelvis

reflect   listening is cessationless end   merge   turn to

Pelvises fascinate me. From the perspective of an illustrator, each animal's pelvis is radically different and specialized. Also, a single pelvis looked at from different angles can appear to be an entirely different bone. From the perspective of life and death, a fractured hip is often the catalyst for an elder living being's decline into death. A broken hip was the beginning of the end of the cat I was grieving while writing this book, and of the aunt whose shell appears alongside "housing crisis."

page 48   "arrived"—human obturator foramen

this hover of still parting

This is the hole or foramen where the obturator attaches to the pelvis. The obturator muscle helps move the thigh. We initiate leaps and steps from the hips and thighs.

The skeleton is made up of necessary holes and other gaps as much as it is of bone tissue. The homeless periods in my life have been painful but formative gaps in the foundation of my history.

page 51   "end of summer"—minnow skeleton

clouds precede invisible rainbows   insects spark storm
untouch one pearl   sounds turn into nothing

I am not sure what kinds of fish I witnessed on the Washington peninsula. In this poem, I refer to slim blue fish, about three to four inches long that swam in great schools, and also to a larger, stout pearly fish, about two feet long.

Although neither fish was a minnow, I chose to draw a minnow skeleton both because minnows are similar in size and shape to

*the small blue fish and because it was the last solid food my cat
would eat before she died. These poems are as much infused
with my feelings for her as with my feelings for the nature of the
area, and my pain of being without a space to properly care for
myself while grieving her and holding down a demanding job.*

page 54   "this here"—human vertebra

sky seems to taper into luster   it leads to this here

page 57   "on the last morning"—found gull feather

emerge dark   go   swallow the sky   in the distance   faint
ghosts beckon

*This poem was written the morning I moved away from
the Washington peninsula and into an apartment in a
faraway town I did not want to live in. Although my bout
of homelessness was about to end, my troubles were not
lessening. They were merely shifting. I was about to spend a
year paying too much for a place no one could thrive in. I was
disheartened, and yet grateful, and full of a sense that there
was some purpose in this tangle of painful experiences.*

page 58   "dear reader"—found stripped shaft of a gull feather

linger outside

*A feather stripped of its flutter cannot enable flight. I am
haunted by the enigma of this de-vaned feather shaft.*

page 60   chambered nautilus with wings

page 61   found shell fragment

*These are two drawings of the same shell fragment. The second
version was drawn during a bout of insomnia in the wee hours
of the night. Because creative work is the most soothing option*

when sleep eludes me, many of the poems in this collection were created or shaped in dim hours by the light of a red headlamp. While a candle illuminated the shell, I used the headlamp to track the development of the ink on the paper.

page 62 found coral fragment

This piece of coral resided among the jagged ballast that covered the patio of my last abode in California. For the five years I lived there, I eyed this piece of ocean with interest, but left it untouched among the rocks. There the coral fragment would have remained if it were not for a kind friend who found it while weeding my patio as I cleaned and packed up my home. In the ensuing events of being unhoused and then housed in a difficult place that did not feel like a home to me, this piece of coral became an icon of the good friends and sense of home I had left behind.

page 63 "dialogues of belonging"—found bird vertebra

I chose this bone for this essay because its foramen looks like a keyhole.

As I grappled with a growing sense that the poems and drawings of this collection alone were not capable of inspiring evolutionary housing equity, I woke from a dream with a question echoing in my head: "Does your art reveal or obscure the truth?" The question followed me like a spectral storm cloud until I decided to write this essay.

Dialogues of Belonging revealed a profound pain I had no idea I was carrying within me. It is not just the pain of my own experiences, but of the experiences of my ancestors, and of the ancestors of the land on which I live.

Come with me,

> *if you would,*

>> *into a loom of mirrors:*

>>> *the essay reveals*

>> *a warp and weft,*

>> *a cloth of histories*

>>> *of people and place*

>> *but it obscures*

>>> *my own story:*

*When I moved from California to Washington state in June
of 2022, I found but one available rental after four months
of searching. I committed to moving in after a video tour, but
upon arriving a month later, I found the rental to be riddled
with black mold the owner did not have the funds to resolve.
I chose not to move in.*

*A kind relative took me in, although her space was not
conducive to cohousing. After another three months of
searching for a rental throughout western Washington,
I signed a year's lease on an overpriced and dysfunctional
apartment because it was all that was available to me.
I relocated to another town, not because I wanted to live
there, but because I needed to live somewhere.*

*This illuminates hidden dimensions of the housing crisis.
Because there is a lack of affordable homes, subpar rentals
that were traditionally listed below market rate are now
priced and rented at or above market rate, and low-income
renters are not able to choose where they live. I had moved*

*to the Washington peninsula to be near a family member
but ended up isolated in a town several hours away.*

*This bout of being unhoused stirred dormant ghosts within me.
I had spent most of my twenties without a home. Challenged
by the overwhelming sensitivities of an undiagnosed
neurodivergence and ill health due to an undiagnosed illness,
I struggled to maintain the basics of a conventional life, and
eclipsed the pain of being unhoused with the extraordinary
escapades of a wild youth. I canoed down the Mississippi
River, rode freight trains, and had a staring contest with a
black bear while backpacking alone and eating only herbs
I found on the trail. Meanwhile, I slept under bridges, on
rooftops, in parks, in abandoned buildings, in odd shacks I
found, and on the floors and couches of friends' houses.*

*Now in middle age, I could still appreciate the singular wonder
of being a porous soul without shelter but I could no longer
ignore the ache of this circumstance, past or present. I am,
however, grateful for this recent ordeal because it sparked
me to look more closely at my own and others' experiences of
homelessness, displacement, belonging, and beliefs around
land ownership.*

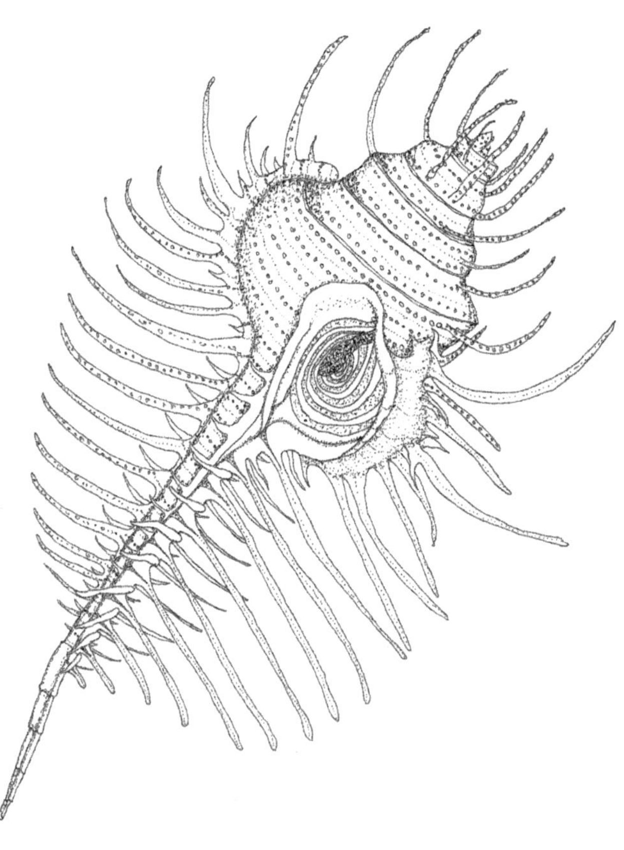

floating in gratitude

thank you to

    Clockhouse for publishing "arrived"

    Miracle Monocle for publishing "blue now"

thank you to

    the Chimakum and Salish lands that birthed this book

    Nina Bailey for finding me through song and continuingcontinuing

    Maw Shein Win for beating the writing drum with me every week

    Emily Moon for deerlike gentleness and charmed resonance

    ash good for precise advice and artful design

    Lauren Paredes for wise and enhancing nudges

    Dianne Diamond for writing back and keeping your door open

    Lee Diamond for grounding presence and generous care

    Ever Jones for quiet strength and support in big pushes

    Kate August for mugwort and coral that guided me through the bardo

    Kristina Clair for a warm puzzle and hops that lifted the crushing weight

    Corinne Manning for eyes that peer in and permeate

    Bianca Maggio and Joe Plotts for ebullience and friendship

    Kay Guyer for happy tales of northern places and plant updates

    Suki O'Kane for rhythm and harmony in myriad spacetimes

    Nancy Beckman for bamboo winds that carried me over unruly seas

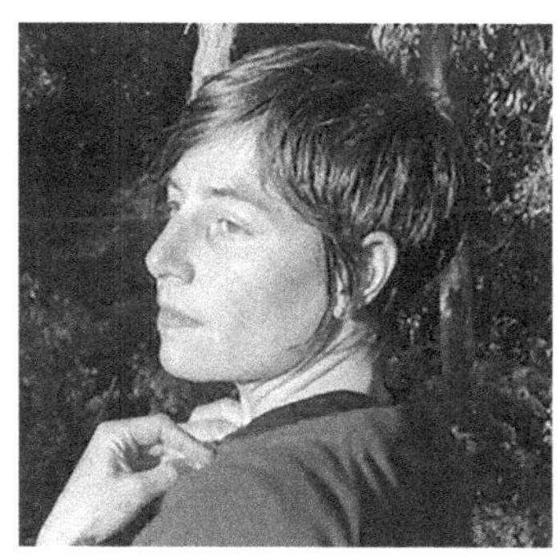

RAE DIAMOND is a neurodivergent interdisciplinary artist, educator, and nature advocate. They wrote, collaged, and published zines as a homeless youth in the '90s, and their poems now appear or are forthcoming in *Petrichor*, *BlazeVOX*, *Clockhouse*, *Miracle Monocle*, and *Sinister Wisdom*. Rae is the author of the prose book, *The Cantigee Oracle* (North Atlantic Books), the founder of the Long Tone Choir, and a lifelong student and teacher of Qigong. Find her online at raediamond.com and @rael3diamond

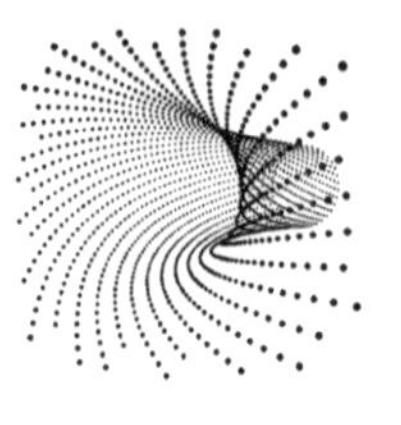

FIRSTMATTERPRESS
Portland, Ore.

First Matter Press is a writers' collective in Portland, Oregon, founded in 2018 to dissolve publication barriers for first-time publishing poets and genre-expanding writers. We invite authors into a creative cohort to crystallize manuscripts in dialogue with editors and fellow writers and collaborate with featured artists on original cover art. We are a 501(c)(3) non-profit organization and our authors maintain 100% of book sale proceeds. Please support independent booksellers by shopping for our titles at Bookshop.org

2023
FEATURED COVER ARTIST LARA ROUSE

FLOATING BONES
rae diamond

TEN-CENT FLOWER & OTHER TERRITORIES
charity e. yoro

OUR FAVORITE PEOPLE IN THE ROOM
edited by ash good, lauren paredes & emily moon

2022
FEATURED COVER ARTIST RACHEL MULDER

BETWEEN THESE BORDERS WANDERS A GOLEM
ahuva s. zaslavsky

EVEN THE AIR, TOO HEAVY
riley danvers

ONE ROW AFTER / BIR SIRA SONRA
sonya wohletz

SOMEONE I CAN HOLD GENTLY
xylophone mykland

STORIES FOR WHEN THE WOLVES ARRIVE
hailey spencer

2021
FEATURED COVER ARTIST ALEKSANDRA APOCALISSE

CONSIDER THE BODY, WINGED
jessica e. pierce

ROUTES BETWEEN RAINDROPS
dan wiencek

THE GROWTH LINES
gabby hancher

2020
FEATURED COVER ARTIST SARA SWOBODA

BODY UNTIL LIGHT
k.m. lighthouse

IT'S JUST YOU & ME, MISS MOON
emily moon

LOVERS AND OTHER STILL CREATURES
eitan codish

2019
FEATURED COVER ARTIST HELLSEA

OTHERWISE, MAGIC
lauren paredes

THE NIGHT SKY IS A PLACE WHERE THINGS GET LOST
andrew chenevert

TIME COUNTS BACKWARD FROM INFINITY
k.m. lighthouse

WE ARE NOT READY FOR WHAT WE ARE
ash good

2018
FEATURED COVER ARTIST HOLGER LIPPMANN

SOUNDS IN MY MÖBIUS MIND
ash good

YOU ARE AN AMBIGUOUS PRONOUN
k.m. lighthouse

FIRSTMATTERPRESS.ORG

www.ingramcontent.com/pod-product-compliance
Lightning Source LLC
Chambersburg PA
CBHW050036040726
47599CB00015B/1710